D1507323

Creative Blogging

For Personal or Business Improvement

"How You Do Dat?"

Paul William Johnson

authorHOUSE®

AuthorHouse™
1663 Liberty Drive, Suite 200
Bloomington, IN 47403
www.authorhouse.com
Phone: 1-800-839-8640

First published by AuthorHouse 1/30/2009

ISBN: 978-1-4389-4995-6 (e)
ISBN: 978-1-4389-4994-9 (sc)
ISBN: 978-1-4389-4993-2 (hc)

Library of Congress Control Number: 2009900453

Printed in the United States of America
Bloomington, Indiana

This book is printed on acid-free paper.

Forward

Paul William Johnson is a modern-day Renaissance man in the most literal sense. He never limits his own potential and has proven again and again that by attuning to intuition and "felt senses," we can truly accomplish anything. Paul is not only an intellectual, but he is also a craftsman. I believe the best illustration of this combination lies in the fifteenth- and sixteenth-century instruments he builds. They serve as embodiments of his aim in this book to merge creativity and intuition with the technical aspects of any task at hand and are artistic masterpieces with pristine functionality. His business acumen, his genuine compassion for others, and his technical knowledge in and experience with several fields of study make him a wonderful ambassador for personal and professional success. He thus practices each and every day everything he advocates, which makes him a model for others to follow in their quests for improvement.

This book frees thinking. For far too long, thinking has been contained by structures and forces – both visible and invisible – that severely limit human potential. Johnson presents salient ideas about how we can use our own thinking productively and collaboratively. He acutely understands the symbiotic relationship between thinking and action, and he teaches us how to tune in to those ideas that, at first, may seem irrational or impossible, but eventually end up taking us to new places in our personal or professional lives. If we attune to these intuitive flashes, as Johnson describes them, we will make better decisions and solve problems more efficiently. He places new and exciting value on the well-known mantra to "keep an open mind" when he writes: "[N]ever in thought acknowledge anything as impossible. When we acknowledge something as impossible, we put our minds in a prison where we are the only inmates. We are then barred from related thoughts, which we cannot now comprehend, that may be possible." If we follow this advice, we will free ourselves from the constraints we place on our own thinking, and we will most likely surprise ourselves with what we accomplish.

Merging intuitive thinking with professional practices works because it acknowledges that the best decisions do not always follow traditional logic; rather, sometimes things *just happen*. We can't quantify an intuitive flash, but we can certainly feel it and act on it. We can't place a traditional methodology onto an intuitive flash, but we can create the best conditions for these flashes to occur. We may not even be able to articulate an intuitive flash, but, if we focus on it, its contents will show up in our actions. These flashes are the seeds that spawn creative intelligence. Contrary to the traditional notion of the genius sitting alone and experiencing an "aha" moment, the intuitive flashes Johnson describes are often most productive in a collaborative setting. He has come up with a way to use new media and the participatory culture of web 2.0 to really reap the benefits of collaborative, intuitive, and creative thinking. By turning to blogs, Johnson shows how groups can go through intuitive thinking processes to come up with the best solutions for issues circulating in any company or work setting. These techniques allow members of the group to truly work together and solve problems in a manner not possible without the technology. They also allow for customer interaction; this is the wave of the future, and Johnson's ideas about intuitive thinking are best realized through the medium of the blog.

As I pondered varying ways to introduce this work, I kept coming back to this: since Paul William Johnson is my father, I have used the ideas in this book (sometimes unknowingly) my entire life; I can't remember a time when I didn't place value on and take pleasure in, simply put, thinking. When I learned as a young adult to tune in to intuitive flashes, place real value on the attribute of patience, and focus my thinking on goals that may at first glance seem out of reach, positive things started happening for me both personally and professionally. Growing up in a household where no dream was too big allowed my far-fetched dreams to be actualized in my adult life. It's never too late to free thinking. This book has something for everyone: whether readers are looking for ways to improve their current jobs, find new jobs, use technology to solve problems, collaborate on a deeper level, or simply find pleasure in everyday life, they will find practical solutions in this book. I can't wait for more people to break out of old, constraining ways of thinking by learning "how you do dat."

Sarah Johnson Arroyo, PhD
California State University, Long Beach

Contents

I. Introduction

There is a story of an immigrant to America who was very successful. He was asked the secret to his success. He said that his father told him before he came to America to keep asking the same question and he would be successful at whatever he tried. This question was "*How* you do dat?" Many books and education systems focus on *what* to do, not *how* to do it. This book focuses on "*how* you do dat." It focuses on *how* to use the blog in a creative way, *how* to use your imagination and intuition, *how* to work in a collaborative group, *how* to find the right job, and *how* to create your own destiny. If you want to improve your business or personal life, please read on. I will show you "*how* you do dat."

Many new ideas are combinations of ideas that already exist. This book discusses the use of blogging combined with creative techniques to improve your personal life or business. The creative techniques discussed in this book were used by me, during a lifetime spent owning and working for large and small businesses as an entrepreneur, a business owner, an employee, and a consultant.

There is a common thread that runs through all creative techniques that can be used to *master any situation*. My grandmother taught me how to find this common thread and apply it to my life. These creative techniques are ageless. To demonstrate this point, I am including in the "Works Consulted" section of this book a list of some of my grandmother's favorite authors who published works in the last half of the 1800's and the first half of the 1900's. She was a great fan of authors such as Frank C. Haddock, Wallace D. Wattles, Prentice Mulford and Albert Einstein. They all knew how to use their intuition to find answers to their questions.

I have experienced business start-ups, a catastrophic business failure, managing a process improvement team in a large public agency, managing a value engineering program that saved $50 million, and participating in or leading value engineering, cost reduction, and process improvement teams. I am also an engineer, a stock and commodity trader, a corn and soybean farmer, and a musician. Through all of these experiences, I have found that Albert Einstein's philosophy works best when applied to creative processes and problem solving. I am using his quotes along with some others to illustrate points in this book. [1]

We cannot solve the significant problems we face at the same level of thinking at which we were when we created the problem. —Albert Einstein

In other words, it is necessary for us to change our thinking and to try different approaches or we will never get different results. Einstein put it yet another way:

Insanity is doing the same thing over and over again and expecting different results.

My intent with this book is to give you some different ideas and approaches that may apply to your specific situations. Some of these ideas might seem a little strange at first, but hear me out and try them. You will then experience their value. Most of the valuable things in life are experiential. What at first may seem like a case of runaway imagination starts to make sense after you have experienced what I'm talking about and can then apply that knowledge to your reality. For example, if you try to tell a young child that she will get burned if she touches a hot stove, she won't have a complete idea of what you are talking about. Once she actually experiences touching a hot stove, she truly understands what it means to get burned. Much of learning what to do is by first experiencing what not to do. Experience has changed her perspective about hot stoves and made her wiser.

When you are courting a nice girl an hour seems like a second. When you sit on a hot stove a second seems like an hour. That's relativity. —Albert Einstein

Once a cat sits on a hot stove, it won't sit on a cold stove either. —Samuel Clemens

Looking back at the life choices we have all made, it is easy to see that most of us have a tendency to pick the hardest way of doing things. We somehow have to touch that hot stove, when everyone tells us we will get burned, in order for it to become part of our reality. Experience is then our teacher and not someone else's words or books. The important thing for us to know is that mistakes are only mistakes if we make them a second time; they are just learning experiences. What we really need to do is take responsibility for our own actions, and if we find that something is not working for us, we need to do something different rather than continuing the same action. This book will show you ways to do things differently in order to master your business, your life, and create your own destiny.

My aim is to open you up to a whole new world of ideas on how to manage and experience your business, your life, and your job. I want to teach you how to think more effectively. This book will focus on how to use the blog in a creative way and how to use the subconscious mind that is in all of us to create your own destiny. In addition, I will teach you how to use these creative techniques in any situation, including stock and commodity trading and even finding the right job.

Our universities are good at teaching students facts and are moving toward teaching students how to think.

The value of an education in a liberal arts college is not the learning of many facts, but the training of the mind to think of something that cannot be learned from textbooks. —Albert Einstein

Indeed, educators are beginning to understand the need to focus more on thinking, and to incorporate learning from experience into their curriculums. This is a good sign, because, as Einstein said:

The only source of knowledge is experience.

Application of knowledge or experience is wisdom, and that is what we need to be successful in our businesses or lives. I have worked with university graduates that have years of education. Some of these highly educated people didn't have the slightest idea how to apply that education. It would be like going into battle with three automatic weapons strapped on your back and not knowing how to use them. This book focuses on personal and business techniques that are part of the wisdom (or application of knowledge) that is necessary to be successful in our fast-moving electronic age. Some of the main topics include

1. Tapping the collective, creative consciousness that's already there inside yourself or your organization;

2. Using creative techniques to improve your personal life or your business;

3. Using the blog in combination with creative processes and techniques;

4. Using different approaches to problem solving in your business or personal life;

5. Using intuition and imagination in any endeavor, including finding the right job;

6. Re-envisioning your approach to natural business cycles, including timing the stock market as a leading indicator of change;

7. Embracing simplicity and intuition in your approach to technology and hiring practices; and using simplicity in any situation, including timing the stock market.

This book will show those wonderfully educated individuals, with these three automatic weapons strapped to their backs, how to use them in the battle of business and life.

If we look at what has been written about Albert Einstein, we will find that most writers tell us their interpretation of what he thought rather than how he thought. This book does the opposite; it focuses on how to think or "how you do dat."

Learning *how* to think as opposed to being told *what* to think is the starting point to getting these three weapons going. We are more often taught what to think by our parents, churches and religious affiliations, schools and universities, news media, and many others. We rarely spend much time learning *how* to think. What many people consider thinking is just parroting some programming that someone else has put into their heads. This so-called thinking is someone else's conclusion. We need to know the how and why of their conclusions before we accept them as our own.

When we are given the conclusions of some authority figure, we often accept them as the truth, even though we don't know how they were reached. When we accept their conclusions as the truth, we are only borrowing or absorbing their ideas. Borrowed ideas are incomplete and inevitably lead us down the wrong path when we try to apply them to different situations. For example, let us look at what the authority figures say about market timing in the stock and commodity markets. I have heard some financial advisors, university professors, and even Warren Buffet state that investors cannot time the stock market and should only use buy-and-hold (hope) techniques. Perhaps the reason they believe and teach that no one can time the stock market is because they don't know "how you do dat." They believe that if market timing is not part of their reality, then no one else can "do dat" either. Sometimes they even collect statistics to back up the erroneous beliefs of their logical, rational minds. What we believe is our reality. Actuality is what is. Will Rogers once said, "It isn't what we don't know that gives us trouble. It's what we know that ain't so." I have used market-timing techniques that follow trends in my stock- and commodity-trading activities for a half century. Market-timing techniques have given me peace of mind and generated enough cash for me to own farms, to own businesses, and to do things that would have been difficult to do on the salary of an engineer. Market timing is part of my belief system and reality because I have experienced "how you do dat." We cannot get anyplace in life without first thinking about *how* to get there. My hope is that this book will help you to be open to experience new realities when you stop depending on others to tell you what to think. Learning *how* to think for yourself will bring you peace of mind and is a necessary step to becoming self-reliant. This will enable you to navigate through any circumstance within which you find yourself.

As long as we are dependent on someone else to borrow his or her ideas or to tell us what to think, we become a slave to that person. I want to help set you free from that kind of slavery with the techniques that I will be presenting in this book. I want you to start using and experiencing these techniques. This will demonstrate to you that there is an enormous amount of freedom, joy, and independence that comes from creative thinking and thinking for yourself.

As previously stated, it takes effort to challenge the status quo and find the path used to get to any conclusion and its origin. There is a story of a young wife who always cut off part of a roast and threw it in the garbage before cooking it. Her husband intuitively knew something wasn't right about this and asked her why she did that. She said that she learned it from her mother. When the husband saw the mother, he asked her why she always cut part of the roast off and threw it away. She said it was because her roasting pan was too small! Understanding the path of events and circumstances will help define the *how* of the conclusion: the real reason why the mother cut off the end of the roast. The choice of paths helps define the *why* of the conclusion: the small roasting pan. Identifying wasteful techniques that have been inadvertently passed down to us is one of the first steps to improve ourselves or any process. Focusing on the *how* and *why* of any conclusion will give us food for thought that can be used with intuition to determine whether the conclusion we are told to believe is correct. Intuition along with thinking is then the application of knowledge.

The intuitive mind is a sacred gift and the rational mind is a faithful servant. We have created a society that honors the servant and has forgotten the gift. —Albert Einstein

Getting a handle on Einstein's notion of intuition as a sacred gift along with the rational mind as a servant is necessary to create or improve anything in business or in life. Honoring and depending on the logical, rational mind or servant while forgetting the sacred gift of intuition is what most of us have been taught to do. This has led to many unsatisfactory results in our businesses and personal lives. Depending first on the intuitive mind or sacred gift, while using the rational mind as the servant, will help us find the right job, the right people, the right business, the right products, the right markets, and the right balance. This sacred gift of intuition and thinking will also help us understand the big picture, understand risk, anticipate change, be in the right place at the right time, and master ourselves and our businesses.

It is better for people to be like the beasts ... they should be more intuitive; they should not be too conscious of what they are doing while they are doing it. —Albert Einstein

Albert Einstein was content to spend an evening with just a pencil and paper and not with books. His logical, rational mind (the servant) was not directly involved in his jotting down the intuitive flashes that popped into his mind. In other words, he had learned how to put his conscious rational mind (the servant) out of the way of that still small intuitive voice (the sacred gift). Einstein looked, heard, and witnessed facts with his logical, rational mind and saw, listened, and comprehended with his intuitive mind. I address techniques in this book on how to use your intuition and thinking in your personal, professional, and business life. If you feel trapped in the same old personal or business issues and need a way out, this book is for you. Let's get started!

"There is a better way to do it. Find it."

—Thomas A. Edison

II. Creative Collective Consciousness

a. What Is the Collective Consciousness?

Collective consciousness can be easily exemplified with the well-publicized story of the hundredth monkey theory. This story demonstrates how the collective consciousness can be used to implement change. The story goes that there was an experiment that involved putting monkeys on two uninhabited islands with no food but potatoes. These islands were far enough apart so that it was impossible for monkeys from one island to get to the other. On one island, the monkeys were taught how to wash their potatoes before they ate them. After the hundredth monkey was taught how to wash his or her potatoes before eating, all the monkeys on the island began washing their potatoes. At the same time, all the monkeys on the island that had never been taught how to wash their potatoes also began washing them.

This same principle has been demonstrated in quantum physics. Fred Allan Wolf, PhD, the popular quantum physicist, says, "I'm talking about global consciousness. I'm talking about the fact that what one being does in some way affects everybody on the whole planet. It's not just separate beings all going their own ways. We are interconnected in ways that are very subtle and not easy to appreciate."

> *A human being is part of a whole, called by us the Universe, a part limited in time and space. He experiences himself, his thoughts and feelings, as something separated from the rest—a kind of optical delusion of his consciousness.* —Albert Einstein

Thoughts from the collective consciousness can also be illustrated by inventions and new discoveries that take place in different countries at the same time and from religions in different parts of the world that have the same stories. Even Buddha was supposedly born of a virgin, and every culture has its wicked witch story. Other thoughts from a collective consciousness might be those that we get from an athletic event, a religious or political rally, the Christmas spirit, and yes, even from any creative collaborative group.

The important point to understand is that our conscious objective minds are not aware that our subconscious minds are all somehow connected like wireless phones. There is a critical mass in change that can happen when a certain number of people change. The change then occurs in everybody. This can work both positively and negatively. It is important for us to focus on positive change and to stop negative change in its tracks. When we began to enhance the creative ability in a small group of people in our organizations, there will come a time when all employees in the organizations will become more creative. This can also be demonstrated by the law of resonance that was discovered by a Dutch scientist who added clocks with pendulums swinging at different beats to the same room as other clocks with pendulums. He noticed that after a short period of time, all the pendulums swung to the same tempo or beat.

Groups of people that spend time together have a tendency to form a collective consciousness that swings to the same beat. They may unconsciously move toward the same beliefs and perspectives on life. This is why we need a variety of perspectives from people who don't usually work together or work in the same field to form an effective creative collaborative team. We will get into the details of selecting a collaborative team later in this book.

Another way to observe how a collective consciousness works is to observe an audience during a lecture and then observe it during a question-and-answer period. You will notice that during a lecture, some of the audience is not focused on the lecturer because there is no mind-to-mind connection. This is especially true when the lecture is read aloud and not spoken extemporaneously. When the question-and-answer period comes along, you will notice an energy level change in the audience when there is mind-to-mind communication between those within the audience and the speaker. You will also notice that many speakers give what may be considered a poor speech until they get to the question-and-answer period where there is mind-to-mind communication. If you are in the audience, you will find that you are thinking many of the same questions that are being asked. Your mind will have connected with the collective consciousness of the group and thought the same question. You will think that the original question was your thought. In actuality, you will not know for sure if the question originated in your mind, in some other mind, or in the collective consciousness of the audience. The benefit of a collaborative process is that it functions mainly on mind-to-mind connections within a collective consciousness.

These illustrations show that there is a great unseen power in a collective consciousness that brings people together to work at the same tempo (pendulum swing) when focusing on common objectives. This power gives the collaborative group greater energy and creative ability to find the best way of solving problems or improving processes. There is a synergism in this process because the group energy and problem-solving ability is greater than the sum of the individual energies.

We can harness this synergized energy of those in the collective consciousness to work for our benefit when we implement creative group processes within our organizations. These creative processes will make our organizations more productive and imaginative as a result of employees engaging in and enjoying their work. Applying these creative processes to collaborative groups helps the employees to learn through cooperation. Cooperation is more powerful than competition because individuals can explore the meaning and significance of their individuality as they contribute to the common whole. Employees should look positively on management's realigned focus on their creative abilities. This management focus on the employees' creative abilities—as opposed to the attitude of what they can get out of them—empowers and inspires everyone in your organization.

The blog on the Internet is the ideal tool that can be used to connect a group of people and use their collective consciousness to create change. Information exchanged on the blog can be adapted to collaborative improvement processes and used to solve problems, improve processes, and implement change. These creative processes can also be used to confirm or find fatal flaws in decisions. Using a step-by-step creative blog process helps the participants to focus on the problem and to engage their intuition.

The blog helps us connect people and speed up the creation of anything, including change, simply by giving it our undivided attention and more directed thought. Most people in business know that they are in the best condition to do their business when their minds can fix themselves on one plan and shut out everything else. Most artists know that they do their best work when their minds are wholly concentrated and absorbed in the work of the minute because this creates an environment for their intuitive processes to work. The step-by-step blog processes discussed later in this book show how to focus the thoughts and energy of each blogger into a collective consciousness that can be accessed by all.

Along with the blog, fostering patience is one of the keys to allowing the intuitive nature of the collective consciousness to really have an impact. The ancient sages said that in addition to time and space, there was a third dimension called patience. They said that a patient attitude was necessary in order to find the dimension where one could access intuition, the flow, or the zone. Athletes are said to be in the zone when playing at their maximum ability. Kobe Bryant didn't think about any shots when he scored forty points in a professional basketball game. He played for the joy of playing and being in the zone. When we are patient, nothing bothers us, we are not over-thinking anything, we are relaxed, and there is no tension in the present. Patience gets us in the flow by not making demands on our rational thinking processes. Freed from the constraints of logical, rational thinking, we can more easily resonate with what we want to accomplish. This is especially true in a collaborative group that has the same desires and passions.

Now let's take a look at what keeps your intuition from working and what you can do differently to make it work. Remember that Einstein said that our society has it backwards when it honors the rational mind (servant) and forgets the intuition (the sacred gift). You have the power to trump society by changing your personal thinking and by making your logical mind your servant. This change happens when you start to use the sacred gift of intuition that Einstein talked about. Complete dependence on logic and using the rational mind has many times led you down the wrong path because it never has enough of the right facts. Using your intuition along with your subordinated rational mind is the key to mastering your life and your businesses. Becoming aware of something that is not working and planning how you could do it differently is the first step to changing your thinking. Otherwise, doing the same thing over and over again and expecting different results is a form of insanity that Albert Einstein pointed out.

Since one learns what to do by first learning what not to do, let's look at intuition killers in more detail. The intuition killer of impatience keeps you in a tense and scattered frame of mind. This shuts down your ability to focus your concentration and use your intuition. Fear and worry are intuition killers because people have a hard time relaxing or focusing their thoughts when worried or fearful. Fear and worry are also the wrong use of imagination, which is part of the intuitive creative process. Another intuition killer is overwork or having nothing in your life but work. For your intuition to work, you need recreation and variety in your life so that you can let go of your thoughts and quiet your mind. When you spend time in two or three areas of outside interest, you can forget all about your work and let go of the work related thoughts. This gives your work mind a chance to rest so that you can receive intuitive flashes. I use music and playing and crafting Renaissance instruments as a distraction to help me let go of my work thoughts.

As previously stated, most people are programmed or trained like slaves to depend on others to do their thinking for them. This could be because they have never understood the need to think for themselves or the freedom that comes when they take responsibility for their thoughts. Learning how to think should be one of our major goals because thinking is what life is all about.

To think is to live. —Cicero

The Internet is a tool that can be used to complement any process. Many individuals have the mistaken idea that finding out what others think on the Internet will tell them what to think and help them get the best answers. It will not! The best answers come from within individuals or groups of individuals through intuitive thinking processes.

"The good news is that the moment you decide what you know is more important than what you have been taught to believe, you will have shifted gears in your quest for abundance. Success comes from within, not from without."
—Ralph Waldo Emerson

b. How to Use Your Intuition to Find Answers to Your Questions

I would like to further explain the creative intuition process that Einstein and others have used. Many of you unknowingly have already used this process. First, you must focus your concentration on the question or issue with the same intensity and passion of an artist. Intensity and passion are easier to generate when you have a strong need or desire to know the answer. Then you must demand and expect an answer from the universe or God or force or whatever your belief system acknowledges as a supreme being. Next you must let go of your thought to the universe and let it find your answer. You then need to engage your mind in some other activity. At a later time, when you are in a quiet or relaxed frame of mind, the answer will pop into your mind.

Some people find it hard to quiet their minds. One fellow told me that he could never quiet his mind except when urinating. That is where his ideas popped into his mind. There are other techniques for distinguishing the endless chain of chatter that goes on in your logical ego mind from your subconscious intuitive mind. All of these other techniques require that you quiet your logical ego mind by relaxation, distraction or meditation. I would like to mention just one of these techniques. If you are not sure that you have quieted your logical ego mind enough to hear that still small voice, you can ask yourself the question, "who?" (Is this logic or intuition?) You may start being able to distinguish that still small intuitive voice when you can compare it to the times the logical mind led you down the wrong path or when the illogical solution, in hindsight, was the best.

However, the easiest technique to master is to stop thinking of the question for which you have demanded to know the answer and do something else. When you least expect it, an intuitive flash will pop into your mind or you will be led to the answer. When you get intuitive flashes, there will be an inner knowing or conviction that the answer is correct. Knowledge that comes from intuition does not require laborious study. In reality, it is simple and requires no study at all.

In your business or your personal life there have probably been times when you were not sure what you should do in a specific situation. Every plan to resolve your issue seemed to be beset with difficulties. When this happens, stop thinking about what to do and do nothing or do something else. Turn the problem over to the master within, the universe or your concept of God and demand that the universe will show you the solution or the best path to take. At some unexpected moment, a person, an intuitive flash or a set of circumstances will arise that solves or eliminates the problem. You may randomly come in contact with the very person you need to carry out your purpose or resolve your issue. You could even see a billboard with a word that answers your question.

On the rare occasion when I could not quickly quiet my conscious logical mind to hear that still small voice of intuition, I would take a dictionary and randomly open it. Within a try or two I could usually find a word that helped to lead me in the right direction. You could try this with a dictionary or any sacred book as a last resort.

Each of us needs to be our own discoverer of which techniques work the best for us since we are all unique individuals that may experience direction from a higher source in different ways. The key to understanding direction from a higher source is that there will be an inner knowing that this is the best way to proceed. Most of us can recall a time when we had a difficult decision to make and had almost given up in despair after worrying, staying awake at night, searching the Internet, thinking it over, and rushing from place to place. After our conscious objective mind became too tired to think any more, the solution popped into our consciousness because that still small voice could finally be heard.

As I have said, tapping the collective consciousness and the intuition of an organization through the Internet can be done with a blog process. Blogs can be applied to processes that are a systematic application of analytical, creative, and evaluation techniques, such as those used in brainstorming, value engineering, and process improvement. They can be customized to fit a particular situation or organization. This approach can be used in any organization to solve specific problems, to reduce costs, to improve processes, or to increase productivity. Productivity drives capital to where it wants to live in our globe. This is the productivity that creates jobs and makes us competitive in a global market. A collaborative blog process can be used as a creative way to improve productivity, to get stakeholders to focus their thoughts, and to collectively cultivate each other's imagination.

c. How to Use Your Imagination to Create What You Want

Let's now look into how the imagination works in general and then develop more specific details that have a practical application. Imagination must be used as a form of constructive thought and not destructive thought. We must always remember that thoughts such as worry and fear are the wrong use of imagination and keep them out of our minds. Every new organization, invention, improvement, construction plan, or any work that was ever done was first created in someone's imagination. We can exercise and expand anyone's imagination by using a blog as part of a creative collaborative process. Using imagination constructively is not daydreaming, but requires effort as anyone who has participated in a brainstorming session will attest. All great things have come from men and women who have had the capacity to think, to imagine, and to make their dreams come true. A collaborative blog process can be used as a forum to create change by increasing an organization's thinking, imaginative, and energizing power.

This energizing and imaginative power of a collaborative group can be demonstrated by watching a group of children playing, compared to an individual child playing alone. The minds of a group of children at play are unconsciously connected in drawing to them a collective current (consciousness) of exhilarating and playful thought. They use their vivid imagination to become so absorbed in their pretend world that they don't even notice the rest of the world around them. Their whole bodies and souls are involved in the group play, as can be seen by their energy level and excitement. Their minds have a marvelous capacity to draw to themselves more life and power from the group collective consciousness. Children playing by themselves are much less energetic and move more slowly.

People, like children, are energized and become more creative and imaginative when having fun in a collaborative group. Being around creative and imaginative people that are having fun stimulates the thinking of those around them. This example of a group of children playing demonstrates the power of focusing our thoughts to create our own reality. Focusing our thoughts and thinking for ourselves is the real business of life; letting other people tell us what to think is *not* the real business of life.

The possibilities for thought training are infinite, its consequence eternal, and yet few take the pains to direct their thinking into channels that will do them good but instead leave all to chance. —Orison Swett Marden

The greatest events of an age are its best thoughts. It is the nature of thought to find its way into action.
—Christian Nestell Bovee

Thought is the property of those only who can entertain it. What is the hardest thing in the world to do? To think.
—Ralph Waldo Emerson

The power to think constructively and deeply and clearly, is an avowed and deadly enemy to mistakes and blunders, superstitions, unscientific theories, irrational beliefs, unbridled enthusiasm, fanaticism. —Frank Channing Haddock

Science is now coming around to the theory that the brain is like a computer and the mind, which functions through the brain, is creative and connected to all other minds. If all minds are connected like cell phones, then it understandable how important it is to get minds to work together by focusing on a creative process such as ones that use collaborative teams and the blog.

Genetically, we are nearly the same as monkeys. The major difference is that the frontal lobes of our brains, where the creative faculties are processed, are much larger. These larger creative faculties give the human an advantage over animals because the human has the ability to change and manipulate his or her environment. In order to change your environment, it is important that you learn how to focus your thoughts through your imagination on what you want rather than what you don't want. This is how you create your future and anything that you want in life. It is amazing to me how many people voluntarily join the monkey troupe and don't even consider using their wonderful creative faculties that give them an advantage in life. Their only experience with these creative faculties is worry, fear, and creating what they do not want, which is the wrong use of imagination.

If we could clock the time we spend focusing on what we *do not* want, we would be amazed at the large percentage of our total waking hours that is spent on thinking about and creating what we *do not* want. It takes constant effort, a positive collaborative team, or possibly a distraction like music to get us out of the habit of creating what we *do not* want in our lives. We also spend an inordinate amount of time with our minds numbed by negative TV or negative news, or plugged into cell phones, the Internet, and computer games. When your mind is numbed out or thinking negatively, it becomes very difficult to use your thoughts and imagination to create what you want. You then easily become depressed and filled with fear and hopelessness because you are drifting in a sea of negativity of what you *do not* want. In this state, it is easy to be programmed and manipulated to serve someone else because you have lost control of your mind.

> *If you don't control your mind, someone else will.*
> *—John Allston*

The drug companies, advertisers, politicians, and many others know very well what John Allston was talking about when they try to program us with fear and take control of our thinking. They try to create a collective consciousness of negativity, worry, and fear to get us to follow their agenda. Franklin Delano Roosevelt understood this when he said, "The only thing to fear is fear itself," because he knew that fear and worry are the wrong uses of imagination. To control fear, we need to take responsibility for our thoughts by making a personal commitment to focus on what we want and not to focus on fear which is what we don't want.

We always have the power to control our reaction to events in our lives even though we may to not always be able to control the events themselves. We need to monitor our thoughts and never underestimate the power that worry, fear and anger have to keep us in quiet despair where depression can enter in and paralyze us. The antidote for this kind paralysis is to have a diversion such as a hobby, to whistle a happy tune, to take a risk or to focus on anything where we can use our thoughts to engage life in a positive way. Tapping the creative portion of our brain by focusing on positive thoughts is the first step to eliminate depression and to improve our state of mind. Most scientists will tell us that we only use 10–15 percent of our available creative mind power. Just think of the unimaginable power that could be released if all the 6.5 billion people on this earth used their minds collectively to create a better world. Recall that Fred Allan Wolf, PhD, the popular quantum physicist, said, "We are interconnected in ways that are very subtle and not easy to appreciate…"

Understanding that we are interconnected gives us incentive to use the positive collective consciousness as a tool to improve our lives and businesses. Exercising the faculties of thinking, imagination, creativity, intuition, etc., in everyone in our organizations will make them stronger and better able to utilize more of their latent power to the benefit of all.

Imagination is more important than knowledge.
—Albert Einstein

I will discuss later how we can develop the imagination of the collective consciousness in a collaborative group. However, I first would like to talk about the details of how the imagination works. This will give you some insight into how to use your imagination both individually and in a collaborative group. Imagination can be used to our benefit or to our detriment. We must always keep in mind that there are destructive ways to use imagination, such as worry, fear, or any form of negative thinking. Your imagination is the tunnel through which your thoughts move to connect with the mind of your creator. These thoughts are then magnified and reflected back to you as your present circumstances. If you use your observation skills, you will see that those around you are experiencing the results of the right and wrong use of imagination by the heaven or hell that they are creating in their present lives. Albert Einstein said, "Logic will take us from A to B while imagination will take us anywhere."

Imagination can only be used in the present. Your present is what you have created with your past thoughts through your imagination. Focusing on past struggles only brings those struggles back into the present. Will Rogers once said, "Don't use yesterday to use up too much of today". Your belief system and thinking has determined your now or present status. Your freedom comes when you realize that you have the ability to create your own destiny and future through the use of your creative imagination. The creative imagination works in conjunction with the subconscious mind. The subconscious mind operates below your waking consciousness and works or creates in reverse to your conscious mind. *The subconscious mind works from effect to cause and not from the cause-to-effect way that your logical conscious mind works.* In other words, if you use your creative imagination to focus on worrying about something, which is an effect, your subconscious mind will draw to you the circumstances (causes) that make the things that you worried about happen to you.

When my business began to fail, I began to worry and use my imagination to focus on the fear of failure (effects). My subconscious then brought to me the causes when every possible thing went wrong. When the business was finally closed down and my money was gone, I had nothing left to worry about! I took with me the experience of the wrong use of imagination and began to use my imagination positively. By using my imagination positively, I found that I could easily surpass anything I could have ever accomplished prior to the experience of the wrong use of imagination. As I have previously stated, we learn best how to do something by first learning how not to do it. It doesn't make any difference if it is life experiences, running a business, or learning how to ride a bicycle by falling a few times.

Most people are taught to believe that "how you do dat" is a step-by-step cause-to-effect process like those found in a cookbook. The "how you do dat" process, when working with the creative imagination and the intuition, is the reverse of cause and effect. You must focus on the effect and let the subconscious mind bring the necessary steps to you, even when you cannot see any physical evidence of your goals being reached. You need to completely believe this process just like you believe that the sun will come up every morning when there is no physical evidence at night that it will come up. If you focus on a logical step-by-step process to get to your goals, you will automatically shut off the many wondrous ways that the subconscious mind and intuition can use to reach your goals. Instead of a step-by-step, logical focus, you must go with the flow and have the mental desire and concentration of a group of children playing. You can then use your imagination to energize those goals so that your subconscious can create the details to bring those goals to you.

Hypnotism works the same effect-to-cause way. Hypnotism is a form of deep relaxation (quieting the objective mind) while maintaining a waking awareness. When we are in a relaxed state, the subconscious mind can be given suggestions (effects) through manipulation of the imagination to create the desired reality (causes). If the subconscious is programmed (cause) by a hypnotist to believe that one is the president of the United States, the person will act (produce effects) just as if he or she was the president. If a hypnotized and blindfolded subject is told that his or her blindfold has been removed (effect) and he or she can read the headlines and stories in a newspaper that is given to him or her, he or she will then be able to read (causes) the newspaper while blindfolded. This is an example of how we are all somehow connected and that the imagination along with the subconscious mind has marvelous and unexplainable creative powers that work from an effect to a cause. Imagining success in any endeavor works the same effect-to-cause way.

Imagination is the beginning of creation. You imagine what you desire, you will what you imagine and at last you create what you will. —George Bernard Shaw

The subconscious mind cannot distinguish between positive or negative and good or bad. Its function is to only bring to you what you imagine, think about, and believe. The secret to making the subconscious mind work for you is to only energize your imagination with the *effects* of what you want.

Knowing how to think and how the subconscious mind works is important to make a collaborative group or our personal lives successful. It is also important to know how the subconscious and the imagination work together when trying to improve your personal life or trying to find the right job. Finding the right job, which I will discuss next, demonstrates the principles of how desire, the imagination, the subconscious mind, and intuition all work together. These same principles apply to collaborative group processes, problem-solving techniques, and process improvement techniques. These principles also apply to any situation where you want to master your life or create your own destiny.

d. How to Use Your Intuition and Your Imagination to Find the Right Job

Now, I will give an example of how to create your own destiny by discussing the detailed principles of how to find the right job. I want to use this example because all of us at one time or another in our careers have experienced looking for and finding the right job.

The first step in finding the right job is to take personal responsibility for your thoughts because they are creative and will attract to you whatever you think about. This process works from effect to cause. When you focus on the job (effect) and let go of the thought, the subconscious will attract to you the circumstances (causes) that will bring you this job.

It may be easier for some of you to comprehend this process if you consider that it is similar to self-hypnotism. Whether you realize it or not, we are all programmed with hypnotic techniques that are sometimes not even comprehended by the programmer. Belief systems of long ago can be programmed by each generation into the next. Repetition is the law of the subconscious mind and is one of the ways the subconscious mind gets programmed. Anything that you hear over and over again will get into your subconscious mind. This repetitive suggestion will be added to your belief system and eventually experienced by you as a truth. Subconscious beliefs can be so strong that they will be vigorously defended and some people may even be willing to defend them with their lives. This is why terrorists can blow themselves up. If parents repeat over and over again that their children are stupid and losers, their children will be stupid and losers when they grow up. We may never know all the hang-ups that have been programmed into us by our parents, religion, schools, friends, etc. However, we do know that we can override that negative programming with the positive creative techniques described in this book. We just need to repeat positive thoughts over and over again along with imagining our goals as already met. These thoughts will then be added to our belief systems and become our dominant thoughts. One of the major reasons why some people have difficulty finding the right job is because of the negative images they have about themselves that were probably programmed into them by somebody else. The techniques in this book will help them change that programming and replace it with the knowledge of the magnificent creative human beings that they really are.

When looking for the right job, you must form a clear picture in your mind of the job you want. You must then focus on this new job with enthusiasm and determination, along with having the positive expectancy that the job will come. This expectancy must be as sure as you are sure that the sun will rise tomorrow. You must make contacts, use the Internet, market yourself, and send out resumes. You must then demand the job and turn the whole process over to your subconscious mind or the master within. If you look at the Lord's Prayer in the Christian Bible, it is full of demands, such as "give us, lead us, and deliver us." This is consistent with "ask and you will receive, seek and you will find, knock and the doors will be opened." I need to emphasize that demanding is a form of prayer and uses a different mindset than the pleading and begging espoused by some religions. Pleading and begging will push the job away from you because it is based on lack and limitation and not having a job. Pleading and begging programs your subconscious mind to set up the circumstances where you will not have a job. The greater the need for the job, the easier it will be to make a positive demand for that job. You can then use your imagination to program your subconscious mind into believing that you already have that job.

The greater the demand that is made for the job to the master within, to God or the universe, the greater will be the force acting through your subconscious mind. This will reduce the time that it takes to attract to you the circumstances you need to get the job. Inspiration, which invents and accomplishes great things, comes through the force of demand. Once you have spent time demanding and picturing the job in your mind, you must let go of those thoughts as Einstein did at the end of his daily work periods. When you let go and go with the flow, you give the universe and subconscious mind a chance to bring to you the details of what you need to get the job. This need may be fulfilled in ways that you may not yet be able to even comprehend.

Imagination is everything. It is the preview of life's coming attractions. -- Albert Einstein

Sometimes, you may not be able to let go of the thoughts or the negative chatter in your logical mind regarding your demand for the job. If this happens, you need to find distractions that will completely absorb your objective consciousness or the right job will never come. I use music and trading to distract and help my objective logical mind let go of my business thoughts. Completely letting go of your needs and desires is the only way they can get to the universal mind. The answers will then come back as intuitive flashes or as a set of circumstances to get you to the right job. This will happen when you are in a relaxed state and not using your logical mind to think about your needs. This is the same way that answers came to Einstein when he patiently waited with a pencil and paper as he relaxed in his favorite chair in the evening. You may also be led to the answers by going with the flow or by having an attitude of nonresistance to the present situation.

This process is like mailing a letter to collect on a winning lottery ticket. If you never let go of the letter in the mailbox, it will never reach its destination and you will never get your lottery pay-out. When you let go of the letter in the mailbox, you will have in your imagination the excitement, the feeling, and the satisfaction of getting that check, even though there are no outward signs that you have it. You don't need to know the exact path the letter takes to get to its destination or the path the letter with the check takes to get back to your mailbox. You automatically imagine, visualize, and have confidence that you will soon go to the mailbox and the check will be there. You believe it will be there with the same belief that you have that the sun will rise tomorrow. One day, you will go to the mailbox and the check will be there! It is just as exciting as you imagined that it would be! When you use this process to find a job, you know that soon you will go to the mailbox and a job offer will be there! It will be just as exciting as you imagined it would be!

It is important that you use your imagination to experience the feeling and satisfaction of the new job even though there are no outward signs that you will have it. You must never use your imagination to focus on fear or worry because you will attract to yourself those things you fear and worry about. You must not permit your objective logical mind to chatter in your head about how the new job should come or why it may never come.

When you go for the interview, you should have the mindset that you will be led to a job where you can make the greatest contribution to your personal growth and to the success of your employer. You will either get an offer for that job or wait for a better job that is certainly on way. When you accept a job offer and let some time pass, you can look back and see how those other jobs that you wanted, and either turned down or didn't get, would not have been as good for you as the job you now have.

There may be obstacles for some of you to be aware of when you use the processes just stated to find the right job or to create what you want in life. You can become your own worst enemy or obstacle by any thought that depreciates your worth, such as thinking that you are not good enough or focusing on why you won't get the job even though you meet the requirements. Focusing on the past in any manner will hold you back or drain your energy. Will Rogers said, "Never let yesterday use up too much of today." Where you have been in the past has no importance when you take a trip. The only thing that is important is where you now are and where you want to go. This applies to any situation in our business or personal lives. Another potential obstacle to consider is that the techniques I have described require effort, mental focus, and discipline to control your thoughts. Many people in our society today have a tendency to be mentally lazy. This is because they have been programmed to seek entertainment, to follow the herd, and to rely on the government or some expert to tell them what to think. The prevailing thinking of many is to look for ways to get something for nothing or with little effort. These mental states must be avoided because they are passive and use very little of our mental creative faculties, which work through active participation.

The only way to get something for nothing is to get or take it from someone who has worked for and earned it or used his or her mind to create it. When wild ducks are fed by humans, they get something for nothing and have much difficulty getting back into the wild and becoming self-reliant. In the same way, humans who don't use their mental capabilities have difficulty becoming self-reliant. Thirty-second sound bites and use of fast-moving electronic devices has programmed many to have very short attention spans. This has led to an epidemic of afflictions like attention deficit disorder that inhibit one's capability to focus their creative faculties on what they want. If we can help those people to begin to use their creative faculties, even in a small way, a whole new world will open up to them. They will then be on their way to creating their own destinies. The most compassionate thing that we can do for our fellow human beings is to give them the tools that will make them self-reliant. This is one of the many objectives of this book. When we deliberately create something in our lives, it will automatically give us the joy of accomplishment and a sense of value and worth.

The human mind has almost unlimited creative ability that improves with every use. It is a magnificently resilient faculty that is waiting for your call to action. It can hardly wait to be taken out of its prison of non-use and be used to create what you want in your life.

In summary, the key to understanding how to find the right job is this: whatever you demand and think about with passion and emotion will be brought to you through your subconscious mind. The whole process starts by first using your creative imagination.

Sean O'Faolain put it another way when he said,

There is only one admirable form of the imagination: the imagination that is so intense that it creates a new reality that makes things happen.

e. Techniques for Improving Your Personal Life and Business

Intense imagination, when combined with other techniques in this book, will create a new reality for you. The more realistic and intense your imagination, the better will be the results. The imagination (the sender) is what sends your desires to the universe through the subconscious mind. Your intuition (the receiver) is how you get the answer back through the subconscious mind as intuitive flashes. The conscious objective mind is used to imagine a descriptive picture of what you want to send to the universe through the subconscious mind and then let it go and go with the flow. Your objective mind is not used to speculate on or to make any effort to influence what the answers will be. Your objective mind must be in a relaxed state or distracted to let the answer pop into your awareness once it is sent. If the endless internal dialogue from your objective mind cannot be stopped, you can try distractive methods such as listening to relaxing music, various forms of exercise, or focusing on something entirely different. Once you have experienced *how* the intuition works, it will be easier to see its benefits. It will then be easier to make a commitment to incorporate these positive creative techniques into your life experience and business processes.

The subconscious mind and creative imagination work the same way in a collaborative group. Each person in the group must use his or her imagination to believe that something is possible when there is no physical evidence that it is possible. When group members use their imaginations to have determination and faith in themselves, they can eliminate any fear or anxiety that they will not succeed. Their imaginations will draw to them, through their subconscious minds, the capacity and power to accomplish the seemingly impossible. This is how victory gets snatched out of the jaws of defeat. This is how people have the power to lift axels or thousand-pound objects off of others in an accident. We must never for a second believe that anything is impossible for us individually or in a collaborative group. This is the cornerstone of success.

When we are in a collaborative team environment, intuitive flashes from the collective consciousness will speak to us in a universal language. Each one of us can then interpret for ourselves the meaning of these intuitive flashes by using our objective consciousness. The universal language of music works the same way. We can all read or play the same notes on any page of music regardless of what language we speak. We can then explain the emotion and feeling of that music in our own languages. This is a crucial concept to understand in order to be successful in our highly technical businesses. The languages of engineers, accountants, customers, clients, and workers are so different that they cannot effectively communicate with each other by only using their objective faculties (five senses). Good communication is necessary to make any business successful. In order to bridge this communication gap, some technical businesses even hire translators to work as a go-between to the various different English language groups within the business. The collective consciousness can be used to bridge this communication gap and eliminate the need for a translator. Since I am a businessman, a trader, a farmer, an engineer, and a musician, let me explain my experiences with the universal language of the collective consciousness while working with different groups. I have noticed that when I have been with a group of construction people, engineers, or musicians, I could sometimes pick up the idea of what they were saying by trying to tune into them instead of focusing on each word to reach a logical conclusion of what they wanted to communicate. Even though they spoke in vastly different versions of English, I could get the idea of what they were saying after just a few words were spoken. This was well before the sentence was completed. I am sure that many of you, in your minds, have completed sentences of others to whom you were closely attuned before they verbally completed the sentences.

I used my intuition to try to find an answer to how this communication worked. The answer that popped into my mind was that this communication was facilitated by the collective consciousness. We all communicate with the collective consciousness in our own languages or versions of English. The collective consciousness then sends a block of information back to us, through our subconscious, that is then interpreted by our objective consciousness in languages and in concepts that we can understand. Any collaborative process that includes people from every level in an organization will automatically and sometimes unknowingly use the collective consciousness to facilitate communication in all their different versions of the English language. It doesn't make any difference if the participants believe in or understand this process. The communication will occur naturally.

One thing I noticed when I was in charge of the cost reduction and process improvement teams for the largest water agency in the world was that I obtained more implementable ideas from internal groups than I did from external groups. I came to the conclusion that there is a collective consciousness already existing in most internal groups that is easier for participants to work though, regardless of the technical version of the English language that they use. Some of the ideas that the group came up with were beyond what I thought were the capabilities of any of the individuals in the group. I have experienced the collective consciousness working in this manner during brainstorming and other creative sessions many times. It is an exhilarating experience that you can also have.

Those whose range of life and interaction with other people is narrow can expand their life experiences by learning how to use their creative imagination. This newfound imagination will contribute to the success of their employer by expanding their experiences and the contributions that they can make. These new experiences can include, among other things, using the blog in a collaborative group setting, which we will discuss later. We have all seen that many people have a tendency to feed off of the same old ideas and thoughts. They use the same old expressions. You can almost tell what canned and worn-out comments will come forth from them in any circumstance. It is like the old LP record that got stuck in one grove and just repeated the same thing over and over again. In a creative process or a successful life, we live and grow largely on ideas. Our minds are stimulated by ideas and the focusing of thought. A creative blog process leads the participants into contact with a variety of people and ever-changing ideas. This produces a far greater range of thought in those that see life as limited and lacking in variety. It would be like the "road to Damascus (seeing the light) experience" that converted the Apostle Paul to Christianity in the Bible. We will all of a sudden see our world differently when we see and interact with other perspectives and ideas. It will then become more difficult to see the world as going to hell in a hand basket. This will help us to find that natural state that Joseph Campbell called "a state of bliss and going with the flow" where it is easier to engage life with positive expectancy. Any forum that helps people engage and interact with others will automatically lead to productivity increases and growth because it stimulates thinking. The collaborative blog is one of these forums.

III. *Using the Blog in Creative Processes*

a. *Combining the Blog with Collaborative Teams*

"Never doubt the power of a small group of people to change the world. Nothing else ever has." —Margaret Mead

"Blog" is an abbreviation for a weblog. The blog format is a series of entries posted to a single page in reverse chronological order. Blogs are generally represented by the personality of the author or reflect the purpose of the web site that hosts the blog. Blogs can also provide links to other sites that support a point being made on a post. Blogs can be used to get people at any level actively involved in the business by participating in a deliberate way.

The Internet is like alcohol in some sense. It accentuates what you would do anyway. If you want to be a loner, you can be more alone. If you want to connect, it makes you easier to connect. —Esther Dyson

Blogs can be used to accentuate a sense of connection to the business. It is a tool to get people involved in the business growth and their personal development. When people are actively involved in a process, they will likely be in the right place at the right time in order to do things with others to meet company and personal objectives. This will give them the experience and satisfaction of knowing that they can make a difference. There is an explosive creative force that can be tapped with a collaborative blog process. This is because it exposes people to the potential for limitless possibilities when there are infinite opportunities for interaction and exchange. Since we are taught *what* to think by mediocre minds and not *how* to think, collaborative blogging is a chance for people to think and use their creative intelligence.

Great spirits have always found violent opposition from mediocrities. The latter cannot understand it when a man does not thoughtlessly submit to hereditary prejudices but honestly and courageously uses his intelligence. —Albert Einstein

The blog facilitates the need of people to use their intelligence to express their innermost thoughts. It gives them a chance to take personal responsibility for their jobs and the success of their companies. They begin to read and hunger for information. This information and involvement makes people more optimistic, self-reliant, progressive, and comfortable with risk. The blog is then a growth tool because it helps people see things differently by expanding their perspectives.

A great thought begins by seeing something differently, with a shift of the mind's eye. —Albert Einstein

Blogs have many applications to businesses both large and small.

When I took office, only high energy physicists had ever heard of what is called the Worldwide Web.... Now even my cat has its own page. —Bill Clinton

Blogs can be used to enhance a business or public agency by soliciting input from employees at all levels on specific issues and changes. The blog can be used to provide the quickest solution, to identify the best course of action on specific issues, and to provide a creative brainstorming process to find new solutions to problems and improve processes. Another application is to use blogs for both internal and external customer feedback. Blogs can be used by entrepreneurs and those starting new business to find out "how you do dat" by connecting them with others who are willing to share their experiences. There are infinite ways to use blogs to improve any situation.

Let's now discuss some of the details of how to use blogs in public and private organizations to improve processes, improve business models, and make communication more efficient. The blog format may be different for a private organization than for a public agency. It will also be different for public comment solicitation, problem solving, and process improvement. In a public agency, the blog can be used to solicit input from the general public to identify potential problems on specific projects and issues. When discussing blogs for private businesses, it needs to be understood that the blog will usually solicit input from only internal employees or a specific talent pool. The bloggers will be required not to identify themselves; this is because in many organizations, people become role identities. When people lose themselves in their role identities, authentic interactive communication becomes impossible. Unidentified bloggers will level the playing field between management and workers and provide for maximum use of imagination without the potential for ridicule. When new blood needs to be introduced into a team, an outside consultant or internal expert from another division of the organization can be used as an anonymous blogger.

The blog can be used to find and focus on specific solutions when the problem is not well defined or understood. For example, suppose that we have a problem that we are not the lowest cost producer of our product. We can set up a brainstorming blog process to only identify potential problems that could keep us from being the lowest cost producer without any discussion or judgment on why these ideas will or will not work. We want to allow all sides of an issue, or pairs of opposites, to exist in equal dignity and worth until the hidden unity can be revealed in the next step. We want to encourage the use of imagination and as many diverse options and possibilities without applying any premature judgment.

Imagination is more important than knowledge. —Albert Einstein

Even so called dumb ideas are encouraged, because a dumb idea may trigger or inspire an intuitive flash in someone else that would lead to a better idea.

*I believe in intuition and inspiration ... At times I feel certain
I am right while not knowing the reason.* —Albert Einstein

The cornerstone to all creative techniques, including brainstorming, is to never in thought acknowledge anything as impossible. When we acknowledge something as impossible, we put our minds in a prison where we are the only inmates. We are then barred from related thoughts, which we cannot now comprehend, that may be possible. Once we think that something is impossible, it will most certainly become impossible in our reality. In actuality, a modification of that thought may be possible or lead to a thought that is possible. The universe cannot bring intuitive ideas into a mind that is imprisoned. It takes effort to keep an open mind when most of us are opinionated and naturally like to defend and debate our positions. Rather than thinking about arguments for or against someone's idea in a brainstorming session, it is better to just consider ourselves observers and only focus on new ideas. We will have a chance to debate ideas in the judgment session, which is a separate activity.

The first step in a creative blogging process is to select a blog facilitator, determine the bloggers, identify the problem or subject, and disseminate information on the subject to the bloggers. After that comes brainstorming. The blog facilitator will screen the brainstorming blogs and give feedback to the bloggers. The next step is a separate blog used to judge these ideas and distill them down to solutions that have the best possibility of working. This gives the bloggers feedback from other bloggers and they become co-creators. Then there is a separate blog used to rank these ideas. The final blog is to find the best way to implement the best solution. Implementation should go smoothly since all stakeholders associated with the change have been part of the process.

A blogging collaborative team needs an internal or external blog facilitator to keep the blog running smoothly. All blogs must be cleared by the blog facilitator before being posted. The facilitator sets the tone of the blog and is responsible for the blog collaborative process, including communicating the ground rules of the blog. The facilitator will temper dominating bloggers and keep the bloggers focused on the problem while working together. The facilitator keeps the blogs positive, provides feedback, and is the only person who can reject a negative or condescending blog. The facilitator is responsible for summarizing the blogs at the end of each step, for posting the next blog, and for writing a final summary of the conclusions and implementation process. Other functions of a blog facilitator include planning the blog process with management, collecting all relative information, and disseminating it to the bloggers. Relative information could include key issues, collecting and distributing cost data, and determining if there are management constraints.

b. Solving Business Problems with Collaborative Teams

There are a wide variety of issues that can be resolved quickly and economically with a blog process. I will list four examples of these processes below with the understanding that there are many different customized processes and different types of teams that could be applied to specific issues and situations.

Problem-Solving Blog Process Example

1. Management agrees to a customized process, type of blogging team, schedule, and cost.
2. A blogging process and team is set up.
3. A blog facilitator is selected to manage the process, cost, and schedule from this point.
4. A blogging team is assembled. This team could be internal, external, companywide, a combination of management and other small groups, or whatever fits the situation. The blogging team needs to keep the blogs confidential and not shared outside the blog group.
5. The bloggers are provided information on the problem: background data, constraints, and ground rules. If the problem is not thoroughly understood, it should be blogged first.
6. Blog the problem. Bloggers identify the problem or potential solutions. There is no judgment or discussion of ideas at this stage. The team needs to include ideas that most people think won't work because most good ideas have been rejected by the masses. Go for number of ideas, considering that if a team thinks it has exhausted all ideas, there still exists 20 percent

more ideas in the blog consciousness that will be the most likely to be implemented. These ideas need to be found.

7. Blog judgment and discussion of ideas from number 6. Reject some solutions; narrow down and prioritize the remaining solutions.

8. Blog implementation of the best solutions in number 7. These solutions must include blogging the advantages and disadvantages of the best solutions. Cost and schedule considerations also need to be included.

9. The blog facilitator drafts a report of recommendations to review with management.

10. The blog facilitator produces a final report incorporating management comments.

Public Comment Blog Process Example

A public agency needs a record of all public comments regarding ordinances, capital projects, and other functions that require public comment. The following steps will establish this record.

1. Management agrees on a customized blogging process.

2. A blog facilitator is selected

3. The public is informed of the blog process and address.

4. The blog facilitator compiles and distributes the comments to the public and public officials for consideration as part of the public record.

Increase Sales Blog Process Example

This example shows the necessity of management input and focus on what is the best subject to be blogged. Assume the objective is to find the lowest common denominator of what drives sales and set up a blog process to increase those sales. Corporations such as GOOGLE derive sales from advertisers based on the number of hits on the site. The blog facilitator would meet with management to get their input and approval to set up a blog process based on increasing the number of hits in various categories instead of increasing the number of advertisers. Management would have to agree that more hits in specific areas would lead to more advertisers willing to spend more advertising money before the blog facilitator proceeds. Management may still want to explore how to find new advertisers with a creative blog process as a separate blogging program. As another option, management might decide to consider a general blog to increase revenues. With these examples, it is easy to see why the creative blogging process needs to be customized to meet the specific cultural requirements and needs of individual organizations.

Blog Help Desk Example

Another application is to use a collaborative blog process as a blog help desk. This help desk could be set up for individual firms to cover a special problem that requires a quick answer. The blog help desk facilitator would engage a prearranged group of experts. In this case, there would be a prearranged talent pool set up that would consist of outside, inside, retired, or a combination of experts in various fields. Answers to the problem could be blogged or separate blogs could be set up for a brainstorming/judgment/implementation/report process. The advantage of this system is that experts from any place in the world can respond in less time and respond with a flexible schedule. Blogs have the ability to facilitate and streamline intuitive and creative processes because when distance doesn't matter, travel cost and the travel time for the talent pool is eliminated.

In general, new business ideas, problem solving, and process improvement can be blogged by tapping a small talent pool or a larger collective consciousness. The basic format would be to identify or state the problem, along with distributing information about the problem. The bloggers would then focus on solutions, using a brainstorming or other creative process. Outside experts from any place in the world can be brought into the blog to bring new ideas and new technology, and to enhance an innovation process. There are limitless ways to use the blog in creative or problem-solving endeavors. Each process should be customized because we and our businesses are all different, and different approaches will work better in specific situations.

The most important benefit of a blog process built around a collaborative group is that the bloggers don't have to be in the same location or time zone. Other benefits are that collaborative team members could be retired employees with specific expertise, internal or external experts, or people from a wide variety of creative experiences. The blog also allows those team members who may not speak up in a group a chance to make a contribution because role identities and strong personalities will be masked. A talent pool could be used that would not otherwise be possible because it could include individuals that have already scheduled part of their time or may be committed part time to other assignments. This process is a methodical approach to implement change. It treats various parts of a problem as interconnected with overlaps and common areas. This process acknowledges interdependencies of team members. Communication is enhanced when boundaries are fuzzy and problems are worked out as a complete set. This process provides for staff upgrade by interaction with experts across the company. It can bring critical issues to the surface more quickly and find overlooked problems in repetitive processes. It can be used as a second opinion on critical issues or confirm the credibility of a potential management decision.

In summary, there are many options to customize the use of blogs and collaborative group processes to fit the protocol and needs of specific organizations. The key to any of these processes is that the bloggers must remain anonymous in order to keep a level playing field and eliminate role identities. Closed blogging processes work best when the blogs are cleared through a blog facilitator. Combining closed blogging processes with creative techniques releases enormous power to solve problems or to improve your business.

IV. Anticipating Change (Cycles)

a. Cycles of change

Collaborative teams can also be used to anticipate change (cycles). The first step is to get the team to start thinking about cycles by giving them some training on how cycles work. Everything in life and business has natural cycles. Even breathing in and out is a cycle. We would die if we could only breath out and never in. There are cycles where human emotion fluctuates between extreme optimism to dire pessimism and then back again. Products have cycles, the stock markets have cycles, the economy has cycles, businesses have cycles, we have a yearly cycle of the earth about the sun, and we even have life cycle costs. In other words, everything in the universe has a cycle. We need to always have a big-picture perspective of our locations on specific cycles and then look at the smaller picture within those cycles in order to find the hidden secrets of cycles.

Italian mathematician Vilfredo Pareto discovered an unequal distribution theory in 1897. The unequal distribution theory says that 20 percent of the parts have a greater impact on the whole than the other 80 percent. Examples of the 80/20 rule are the following: The stock market trends only about 20 percent of the time; 20 percent of the people in an organization, public or private, will usually do 80 percent of the productive work or account for 80 percent of the profits. In a cost reduction process, we should focus on the 20 percent of the items that make up 80 percent of the cost. You can use this 80/20 application in almost any area of your business to make it run more smoothly and generate more profits.

There is a fast change characteristic of the 80/20 rule that is a hidden secret and not usually discussed with this theory. This characteristic says that change in a business happens quickly and uses only 20 percent of the total cycle. The hidden secret for an entrepreneur or businessman is to consider that one of his or her more important functions is to anticipate change because it comes quickly. This can be demonstrated by taking a nontraditional look at cycles by recalling, in your mind's eye, a picture of a sine curve. You will remember that a normal sine curve spends about 80 percent of the time above or below the middle of the range. The sine curve spends only 20 percent of the time traveling between these extremes. This tells us many things, but the hidden secret is that change happens quickly. It is difficult to adjust to change unless management has a process in place to anticipate change and implement adjustments to that change in the shortest possible time.

Tapping the collective consciousness of the organization with a blog process is one of the best ways to anticipate and adjust to change. When you get your whole organization involved in anticipating change, it can be an advantage that it happens quickly. When planning products, a good entrepreneur spends time on finding products or services that are in different phases of their product or individual cycles. Why not get your whole organization involved in finding new products? The sport utility vehicle has a different product cycle than a fuel-efficient car. Many cycles are interdependent. For example, let's look at all the many businesses that cycle along with housing starts. These businesses began to fail with a decrease in housing starts because their owners did not spend time looking for products or services with different cycles or anticipating a quick cycle change. The tools in this book can help you get your organization involved in finding products with different cycles and anticipating change. This will make change happen naturally and not catastrophically.

As previously stated, one of the main functions of the person in charge of his or her business is to anticipate change. Businesses that anticipate cycle changes will spend more time changing products or reducing forces and costs before a change/downturn begins. Again, tapping the collective consciousness of your organization with a collaborative blog process will help anticipate and adjust to these changes. This process can also be used to get your business in shape for the next cycle or product upturn if your business has not been able to find products or services with different cycles. When costs are reduced faster than a business slows down, receivables and payables will go down while cash will go up. Saving this cash makes the business stronger and in a better position to take advantage of future opportunities.

Cycles are a naturally occurring event and give businesses an opportunity to replace, re-employ, or re-educate some of the 80 percent of the people and products that do not add to profits or are non-productive. The way to get these 80 percent of unproductive people excited about their jobs and producing profits is to get them involved in a collaborative blog process where they have the freedom to express themselves.

Everything that is really great and inspiring is created by the individual who can labor in freedom. —Albert Einstein

b. *Growth versus Efficiency Cycles*

Another part of a cycle that is worth mentioning, especially for small businesses, is the transition between the growth cycle and the efficiency cycle. There are also personal growth and efficiency cycles. The growth cycle is where the prime emphasis is on growing the business. The business then hits an inflection point in the cycle where too much expansion and growth would destroy the business because inefficiency is creeping in. At this inflection point, the focus needs to be changed to how to consolidate and run the business more efficiently. If a manager has anticipated this change or a market downturn, he or she can begin implementation of the efficiency part of the cycle while the business is still expanding. During the efficiency phase, the manager needs to be anticipating the next business upturn and the cycle goes on and on. This same growth/efficiency cycle can apply to a public agency that has a large one-time increase in its capital improvement program and employee requirements. Once this large project is completed, there are layoffs because of reduced employment requirements. Anticipating these changes can make the cost and transition to this cycle much easier to manage.

Now, I would like to cover cycle experiences I have had with businesses that I have owned and/or managed. I will give examples of change that came quickly and examples of a growth/efficiency cycle. The first example is a startup business that focused on a niche market. We made exceptional profits the first three years after we started the business. We focused on growth rather than efficiency during this period. We did reach a point where we could not maintain the rate of growth, and all of a sudden, efficiency became the most important issue because our profits and cash flow were drying up. We had too many people when our growth rate started to slow down. I was reluctant to get rid of them because good technical people were hard to find. As the profits evaporated, I was forced to get rid of these people anyway. The lesson for me was to run the business first and then focus on providing jobs for good productive people. If I had anticipated the slowdown in growth and began making efficiency adjustments earlier, some of those good technical people that I had to lay off would have still had jobs and would have been ready for the next upturn.

Have you ever noticed that birds of a feather flock together? Another company I owned was very profitable for the first four years into an expansion phase. I was not careful enough about considering the creation of a positive work environment along with understanding the inner attitudes of some of the people I put into management positions. I just hired people with good experience because I needed them and they were available. I ended up with too many people that hated their jobs and worked for me just because they needed high-paying jobs to subsidize their lifestyles. People that hate their jobs usually have family, financial, and personal problems. It is then potentially possible for them to have more difficulty taking responsibility for their lives and their jobs. My managers hired people just like themselves. Workman's compensation claims began to rise and other employee problems flourished. When I needed my management/employee support to change to an efficiency mode of operation, they only knew how to focus on problems and not solutions.

I could have avoided this had I understood my managers as individuals—how well they complemented each other, their ability to be flexible under the stress of change, and their ability to work in collaborative groups—before I hired them. I placed managers that had the right experience into jobs they hated, and change happened quickly on the downside once things started to go wrong. I think it is important to keep on the lookout for any disgruntled employees or managers and get to the bottom of any dissatisfaction as soon as possible. The cockroach theory says that when you see one cockroach, there will always be more. By initially thinking the one case of dissatisfaction was only an anomaly, I ended up with a whole colony of cockroaches. My only alternative was to close the business down because I did not have a base of management/employees that could help me manage change or change to an efficiency-oriented business program. From that point on, it became clear to me that understanding the complete person that I hired was an essential part of any successful expansion. It was even more important than focusing on potential profits from expansion.

In the old paradigm, financial background, workman's compensation history, traffic violations, drug testing, felonies, and misdemeanors were just as important as work history and references. In the new paradigm, if we can understand our people as individuals rather than faces with certain verifiable backgrounds, we will have the tools to get them into a position where they can make a positive contribution, or we should not hire them at all. This new paradigm also underscores the idea of the importance of creating a work environment where people love and enjoy their jobs. When the employer can cultivate a group of people that are positively stimulated by and love their jobs, a critical mass will be reached and the entire group will be stimulated by and love their jobs. Looking back at my business failure, I can now see that my major problem was that I created a critical mass of people who hated their jobs and then I had a company where everyone hated their jobs. From that point on, everything possible went wrong. This underscores the importance of selecting positive people and creating a work environment where they love their jobs. We will then reach a critical mass where everything goes right and providence falls in our path.

c. *Personal Financial Cycles*

Individuals have cash flow/growth cycles where investments pay off, salaries increase, and their personal net worth grows almost effortlessly. These are usually followed by consolidations that require an adjustment in lifestyle such as focusing on needs rather than wants. If too much debt is accumulated during the expansion period, then debt has to be liquidated at great pain and expense during the downturn. If individuals or businesses saved the first 10 percent of their earnings, then they would be amazed at how fast the law of compounding works for them instead of against them, as it does when they have debt. The 10 percent savings would have generated literally millions of dollars for them by the law of compounding. These individuals and businesses would then have a plan to ride out any changes in the individual or business cash flow cycle. Albert Einstein was asked if he believed in miracles. He said, "Yes, I believe in the miracle of compound interest."

A good goal for most individuals would be to earn more from the money that works for them than they could make working. At this point, they are free from the indentured servant trap that keeps them working to pay off debt and to keep food on the table.

It is not the money you work for that is important; it is the money that works for you. —Wallace D. Wattles

d. Stock Market Cycles

The stock market has long-term and short-term cycles. We have to be careful to always keep the long-term cycle in focus and not project the last short-term cycle into the long term. For example, as long as the long-term cycle is up, the short-term cycle has a high probability of recovering to new highs. This is when buying dips and dollar cost averaging works. When the long-term cycle is down, we should avoid the long side of stocks because there is a high probability that most stocks will continue to go lower. If we want to be aggressive and stay in the stock market, we should sell into stock market rallies and should not do "dollar cost averaging", which is averaging a losing game. I will show you a technique to determine if the long term stock market cycle is up or down in the chapter on "A Simple Technique for Timing the Stock Market". Cash is usually king in a down or bear market because cash purchasing power increases through deflation. This translates into an enormous return when you consider that you can buy more of almost anything with your cash at a lower price during deflationary periods. However, we must always be on the alert for the cycle change from deflation to inflation.

The debt-based monetary system used in the United States and other countries needs inflation to function because the debt is managed by being inflated away every twenty years or so. We should look for the government to reintroduce inflation during deflationary periods by printing more money. We can use the intuitive techniques described in this book if we are not sure what our logical objective minds are telling us about our locations in the stock market cycle or the deflation/inflation cycle.

e. Debt Cycles

There are also debt cycles. Our modern worldwide banking system is electronically interconnected and works like a collective consciousness. Excessive money creation has made vast amounts of nearly free money available to the banking system. This has enticed banks to make marginal loans that cannot now be paid back. We have just gone through a debt expansion cycle and we are in a debt contraction cycle. Excessive debt is now common throughout the world and is choking off the world's economies. The bank problems, stock market decline, and personal bankruptcies demonstrate the consequences of the excessive use of debt and leverage. We are now in a business and stock market down cycle. It will take new approaches and time to get the collective consciousness of the worldwide, interconnected banking system working again. When the excesses of the last up cycle are corrected with a down cycle, a new up cycle will begin. There is no better way to get through a down cycle than to use the power of the collective consciousness and collaborative teams within your organization to find opportunities for change and cost reduction or process improvement.

Managing debt is the final point I would like to make regarding cycles. The best way to manage debt is to pay it down as fast as you can when a business or your personal life is in the expansion phase. This will make future interruptions in cash flow easier to handle.

In any business or in our personal lives, we should take cash from our good times and pay down debt because debt has the potential to destroy our lives or businesses. When the individual or business debt limits are reached, any interruptions in cash flow will make it difficult to make current debt amortization payments. A good contingency plan for this occurrence is a must if any expansion cycle is financed with debt. Debt is not a mortgage on a business or house or car. It is clearly a mortgage on your future earnings, whether for a business or an individual. In order to reduce the probability of ruin caused by debt, businesses can expand at a slower rate without or with minimal debt. Yes, interest rates have a cycle. It looks like we are now in the bottom of the interest rate cycle and we need to anticipate that higher interest rates could come sometime in the future. Now is the time to pay down any debt and accumulate a cash reserve. Then credit lines will not have to be used when interest rates are higher.

We need to keep an awareness of where we are in all cycles, big and small. This awareness will reduce the cycle impact on our business or personal lives and give us opportunities for change. These opportunities for change can be enhanced by using the blog and collaborative teams to awaken our creative abilities. It is when we embrace and anticipate change that we can find new opportunities that change can bring. Involvement in a collaborative blog process is a way to teach others about the knowledge that comes from the collective consciousness of your business through intuition. This will awaken the joy of creative expression that will lead to new opportunities and positive change for your business.

It is the supreme art of the teacher to awaken joy in creative expression and knowledge. —Albert Einstein

Understanding how cycles work in your personal or business life helps you to reduce worry and fear of the future. Then you can use your intuitive faculties for guidance. Worry and fear of the future should be avoided at all cost because they are the wrong use of imagination and cause your intuitive faculties to work against you. Will Rogers said, "Worry is like paying a debt that may never come due". Understanding the rhythm of cycles can give you a roadmap that helps you get where you want to go. When used along with your intuitive faculties, you then have the key to create your own destiny.

V. _Keeping It Simple_

a. Two-Edged Sword of Technology

Technology is a two-edged sword. We must balance too much information versus using only the right information and keeping the decision-making process simple. The Internet has made so much free information available on any issue that our logical minds think they have to consider all of it in order to make a decision. We then become stuck on a mouse wheel of looking for answers. This makes us information blinded, like deer in headlights, when trying to make personal, business, or other decisions. To be successful in anything today, we have to keep in mind that in the land of the blind, a one-eyed bandit can accomplish the seemingly impossible. The one-eyed bandit understands the power of keeping any analysis simple and will be the undisputed king when he uses his one eye of intuition.

Any intelligent fool can make things bigger and more complex... It takes a touch of genius – and a lot of courage to move in the opposite direction. **—Albert Einstein**

Thinking that the more free information you get from the Internet, the better decisions you can make leads to an information age infliction called gridlock of the mind. This infliction causes insomnia, hypertension, fear of making a mistake, and plain old anxiety. If you resist over-thinking and over-searching on the Internet, you will never have to experience gridlock of the mind

Sometimes one pays most for the things one gets for nothing.
—Albert Einstein

This book has shown you how to go with your intuition or first impression and know that the first thoughts and simplest solutions are always the best.

b. *Simplify, Simplify, Simplify ...*

Occam's Razor

William of Occam (1300–1349), an English logician, propounded Occam's Razor ... A paraphrase of the Latin translation is: The fewest assumptions a phenomenon depends upon, the better it is. In other words, the simplest system is more likely to be correct.

Everything should be made as simple as possible, but not simpler. God always takes the simplest way.—Albert Einstein

If you are struggling in your business or personal life, and if you feel stressed and tired out, just begin to simplify your processes. Get rid of the things that don't support your goals or objectives. Close out friends and associates who are not positive; this includes whiners. Stop over-committing and volunteering for too many activities that provide for the needs of others. Focus more on your needs, your family, and the simple things that are most important to you. Then your life will be simply magnificent. Your creative ability flourishes in a relaxed atmosphere. Using intuition is not a grueling sweat-of-the-brow process, but is the simplest and most powerful process that takes the least amount of time when your thoughts are focused.

Examples of how to use your intuition are provided throughout this book. The process is simple but bears repeating. Focus your thoughts on a question; demand and expect an answer; let go of the thought to the universe; do something else. Relax, and at some point, when the endless chain of thoughts stops in your head, the answer will pop into your mind and you will have an inner conviction that it is correct.

The Internet is an excellent resource for getting information and connecting people but is not a good a tool for decision making. When the Internet is used as an extension of the logical mind to find convincing proof of a certain outcome before a decision is made, we get right back on the mouse wheel because the logical mind will always need more proof. The Internet's greatest power comes when it is used to connect people so that their minds can work as a collective consciousness. The blog systems mentioned in this book are the path to the future. Other greater systems will evolve in the future since the possibilities of using the blog along with the collaborative collective consciousness are infinite.

The stock market is another example of a collective consciousness that is moved by the collective perception of events rather than by the events themselves. Now, let's talk about how to tap into this collective consciousness with a simple stock market timing technique to find out where we are in an economic cycle.

c. *A Simple Technique to Time the Stock Market*

Stock market timing techniques can be as simple as observing the one–hundred- and two-hundred-day moving average of the price. There are many free charting services available on the Internet that will give you moving averages. These charting services also have a whole basketful of technical indicators that make market timing complicated because they will distract you from the big picture. Ignore these technical indicators and look only at the one-hundred- and two-hundred-day moving averages. As long as the one-hundred-day moving average is above the two-hundred-day moving average, the trend is up and you can buy dips.

At some point, the one-hundred-day moving average will cross below the two-hundred-day moving average. This is called the death cross and will signal a change in the collective market consciousness or market sentiment from bullish to bearish while the outward signs are still bullish. You will notice that the stock market will begin to have a tendency to go down instead of up on good news. This signal is called a death cross because it has a high probability of being the death of the up cycle and the beginning of the down cycle or trend. Get out of stocks. If you want to be aggressive get short socks. Stay out of long positions in stocks until the one-hundred-day moving average again crosses above the two-hundred-day moving average. If you had used this simple technique, you would have missed the great bear markets of the past century. Your dollar return would be many multiples of what it would have been if you had adopted the buy-and-hold or hope philosophy.

I must tell you that I only trade for my own account and am not a registered financial advisor. Therefore, I cannot legally give investment advice. My intention with this book is not to tell you *what* to buy or sell, but to give you the necessary tools so that you can learn *how* to think for yourself as to where to invest your money. I also want to help you to understand the importance of learning how to make your own investment decisions. After all, what are we here for except to have fun deliberately creating what we want in life and growing in wisdom and understanding from our learning experiences? If you are in a quandary over what to do with your investments, your sacred gift of intuition can always be consulted.

If you are a manager in a business and start seeing a death cross in the major stock market indexes, you will have an advance signal that the expansion phase is ending because the stock market is a leading business cycle change indicator. Get ready for the business contraction phase that is about to begin, even though times are still good. There are other techniques to determine long and short term trend changes, but I wanted to focus on the death cross because it is the simplest and easiest for anyone to follow and understand.

If you are working and observe a death cross in the stock market, make sure that you are in a job where there is a low probability of getting laid off. You might want to consider getting some training or finding a job that is more recession proof. This is the time to pay down debt, conserve cash and sell assets that are leveraged. This is also the time to get your collaborative teams together to find ways to minimize the effects of the contraction on your company. The down cycle will reverse at some point when everyone thinks that there is no hope and the one-hundred-day moving average will again move above the two-hundred-day moving average. When this happens, start getting ready for the next up cycle and get your collaborative teams involved in finding new markets and opportunities.

Many human beings exhibit a tendency to follow the herd. Using the herd instinct, instead of thinking with the mind, is what the herd or majority does. The herd never leads. It just follows. No original or creative thoughts ever come out of the herd. They just parrot what someone else has said or programmed into their minds. Let's take a look at how the herd instinct works in the stock market. People are like sheep; they feel a sense of security by being in a herd. They feel more comfortable buying a stock or commodity that brokers or analysts have recommended as a buy and hold. They are programmed into believing that a broker knows more than they can possibly know about stocks and accept his or her conclusions and recommendations without question. If they would have just thought for themselves and looked back at some of the broker's previous recommendations, they would have discovered that many times they would have done better by doing the opposite of what the broker recommended. Even when the broker was right and they had a profit, they sometimes times gave it all back on the next down turn because they had no plan to take a profit and ring the cash register.

The market timing techniques I use work for me because, before the trade is made, I have a maximum loss point or stop to get out if I am wrong. My market timing techniques also have a profit objective or a plan to take profits if the trade works in my favor. I will not make a trade unless the potential profit is five times the potential loss. This way, I can be right less than half the time and still make a profit. The only reason to get into a stock is to make a profit! The only way to make a profit is to sell the stock. Buy-and-hold or hope techniques have no plan to sell the stock and make a profit. The buy and hold plan is to ride the stock up and down for the long term. If the company doesn't go broke in the meantime, the buy-and-holders hope that the stock will show a profit when the money is needed. World War II baby boomers now reaching retirement age are finding out that because they had no plan to take a profit, they don't have enough money in their 401Ks to retire. They are in this predicament because they have never learned *how to think* for themselves in regards to their finances. This example shows the difficulties that can occur when we accept and believe the so-called experts when they tell us *what to think.*

There is another important reason that I determine my maximum acceptable loss in advance of a trade. The reason is that when I reach the maximum acceptable loss in my trade, the premise for my trade is wrong and I get out of the trade with a small loss. I have been given the opportunity to admit that I am wrong. This is okay, because my plan is to take small losses until I can find a large win. Remember that I have demonstrated that we learn how to do things right by first doing them wrong. Buy-and-hold techniques never give us a clue as to when we are wrong because the herd always thinks that the stock will be higher in a few years. It is too late to find out that we are wrong when the company goes out of business, the stock loses most of its value, or the stock has gone down when we need the money. With the buy-and-hold strategy, we never have opportunities to learn or to have any power over our circumstances because we have to helplessly worry and watch our accounts go down and hope they will recover. Hope has never been a good paymaster for me. Buy-and-hold or hope strategy hasn't worked for me because it doesn't give me a signal when to get out of a stock to minimize my losses and admit that I am wrong or have a plan to make a profit by selling a stock.

Buy-and-hold techniques sometimes use dollar cost averaging to buy more stock as the stock goes lower. Dollar cost averaging sometimes works in a long-term uptrend and it fools people into believing that it will work all the time, including a long-term down trend. Dollar cost averaging has the fatal flaw of not limiting losses, not telling us when we are wrong, and not letting us know where and when to take a profit. In addition, it is usually trading against the trend. My experience has been that the best way to add to a position is to do the opposite of dollar cost averaging. I buy more of a stock as the stock goes up because I am trading with the trend. I then move my sell points up as the stock goes up in order to lock in my profits.

The old time traders such as Jesse Livermore said that the biggest speculative blunder of all is trying to average a losing game. They understood that once a stock starts going down, it could go to zero or they may end up magnifying their losses. Some of the automobile stocks that lost most of their value in 2008 are good examples of this.

There is an inner peace that comes with using market timing techniques because I know that I can learn from my mistakes and adjust my trading plan when I am wrong. Small losses will keep me in the game and are part of my plan to win. Combining these learning experiences with the tools that have worked in the past gives me confidence that I will catch a move that makes profit. The profits along with my learning experience give me the incentive to keep going until I reach my yearly goal.

It is never too late to start using a trading plan along with your intuition for guidance. Then you won't have to rely on the herd or a broker for advice. You will become master of your finances, your job, and your life when you learn how to use, control, and direct your thoughts to create what you want. This gives you power over any circumstance. The only loss you will ever have is when you lose your limitations, your weaknesses, and the calamities that you have created for yourself by the wrong use of imagination and thinking.

d. Selecting Your Collaborative Team

Most of us have hired many people based on human resources criteria along with some technical and personal information that the boss thought was important. I have found that most people like to hire people just like themselves. This may have worked in the past, but today, with interconnected team processes, we don't want all people who are the same. Some need to be leaders, some need to be doers, some need to provide creative strengths, some need to be inspirers, some need to provide enthusiasm, some need to provide imagination, and so on ... In other words, we are looking for a diversified team where members complement one another. When putting together a new team or hiring team members, we need to look at each individual and how he or she fits into the whole of our team objective. When using a team from the entire organization, we have to play with the cards that have been dealt to us. The bigger the team, the more possibilities exist for diversity.

In my experience, the real reason that most problem employees have been fired or replaced is because of interpersonal problems or their inability to take responsibility and accountability for their jobs. These problem employees tend to be the people that were hired because of their outstanding technical abilities. I have seen very few people who have been fired because of a lack of technical competence, yet technical competence is near the top of many job descriptions.

There is a better way to hire the right people. We all see our world through the spectacles of our thoughts. It doesn't take long to determine if people's thoughts are predominantly negative or positive, victim or victor, happy or depressing. Positive people succeed best in a team environment. Those that don't succeed are those that get involved in personality conflicts; are domineering, demeaning gossipers; and a whole list of traits that most would consider attitude problems. Negative people with negative responses to their life experiences sometimes project this negativity on those around them and can create a malaise in the workplace. They are usually fault finding and full of cynicism and prejudice.

Positive team members are more receptive to new ideas and prone to consider wild and extravagant ideas as stepping-stones to great ideas. They will understand that what they think is unreasonable may be reasonable to someone else, or vice versa. There may be situations where we want every stakeholder and employee to be involved in the collaborative team process. In that case, the team may need some training in creative thinking. An example of an item that could be included in the training is the importance of open-mindedness because anyone who thinks that something is impossible will make it impossible for themselves. We are taught by our society to find out why ideas won't work or what is wrong with the ideas rather than what is right about them. The team needs to understand that their mental focus needs to change from why something won't work to why it will work. In other words, the team needs to take on the role of an optimist in any brainstorming process.

The optimist believes the best in all possible worlds and the pessimist is afraid the optimist is right. —Old saying

A specific trait that must be found or developed or cultivated in at least one team member is that of an inspirer, someone who has the capacity to stimulate others into creative thought. These individuals have a natural ability to project the thought of comfort, cheer, admiration, strength and new ideas to others. Thought has power to work results in proportion to the amount of demand or intensity and focus put into it. The inspiration that creates great things comes through this demand and focus. Inspiration came to Einstein as self-evident ideas after he had focused on questions and then let go of thinking about them. He said that these ideas just came to him and he could not tell how they were made.

Intuition has worked in ancient through modern times in the same unchangeable way as mentioned in this book. The inspired power of an idea acted on by individuals or collaborative teams will naturally demand expression in some material form. Such thoughts give the inspired individual no rest until they commence working them out in material form. All the great inventions in our world came this way.

A collaborative team that is focused on a common objective will draw to themselves new ideas. This is an exciting and exhilarating experience that gives the team members new life that comes from a state of continuous variety. The team members' minds are then opened in the right direction, and imagination and intuition have a chance to begin to work. It is important that we start a team with a nucleus of creative, quality people. These people will then help attract others of a like mind.

The following are some questions that could be used in the interview process to select a collaborative team. These sample questions can be used to determine what role a person might play in a team and if they would be compatible with a creative collaborative process. Some people are excellent interviewers and have all the buzzwords, but your intuition will tell you that they may not be right for the team. It is more important to know how people think about themselves and their world, rather than what they have done. Most things that we have done are just history, and hopefully, we are different, more adaptable, and more evolved people than when we did the things in our past. When your intuition gives you an uneasy feeling about a potential team member he or she should be rejected. It is important to avoid any potential team member who has a tendency for pettiness, blaming, complaining, and accusing, or an affinity for creating drama and conflict in a team environment.

Since I am covering a wide variety of uses for collaborative processes, I will give some general interview questions with the understanding that you could customize questions for a specific process.

1. How would you describe yourself without referring to your job?
2. Explain any experience or association you have had with theater, music, or the arts.
3. What are some things that upset and disturb you?
4. I shine and am most happy when _____.
5. I excel at _____. This is or is not one of my passions.
6. What I do most effortlessly is _____.
7. I like to play the _____ role or roles on a team (examples: leader, doer, inspirer, creative, big picture, detail, etc.).
8. I would like to now have more _____ (examples: humility, courage, leadership ability, tolerance, ability to make more people laugh, creativity, patience, enthusiasm, and change).
9. What are your passions?
10. What innovative ideas have you had that excited you?
11. What achievements have you had that you are most proud of?
12. Do you feel comfortable taking risks? What kind of risks are they?

13. Tell me about the time you took a risk and the outcome.
14. Would you prefer to work with others or by yourself?
15. Have you ever worked in a collaborative team or process? If so, what role did you play?
16. Tell me about the most fun you have ever had.

These or similar interview questions will give you an indication of how potential blog team members will function or fit in a collaborative team environment.

One of the most difficult collaborative team members that I have ever worked with was a chief engineer from a major engineering firm. He couldn't follow the brainstorming process and said that he had tried any idea that came up and it didn't work. He never could understand that we did the judging in the judgment phase because his ego blinded him into thinking that he was the final word on any subject. This man held a high position in a private engineering firm, yet could not function in a collaborative team environment. We need to know how flexible and open-minded a team member can be.

e. How to Function in a Collaborative Team

In order to function in a collaborative team, the team member needs to be able to focus on why something could work rather that why it won't work. Looking first at why something won't work or what is wrong with it has been programmed into all of us. This is the root cause of most interpersonal conflict and drama and why our creative faculties won't work for us. Just notice that when you want to try something new, the herd will immediately tell you what is wrong with it or why it won't work. People that have accomplished anything in life have had to discount the advice of the herd. Well-functioning collaborative team members will focus on the unique capabilities of each individual on the team and why any new idea might work.

Collaborative team members need to be passionate about the tasks at hand. When we become passionate about doing something, all the details needed to get us to where we want to go just fall in place. I have noticed that passionate people on a creative team are always having fun and do not consider what they are doing work. Fun indicates enjoyment and a prevailing mood or frame of mind that is confident, determined, and serene. In the game of golf, Jack Nicholas said, "People do their best at things they truly enjoy; the game is meant to be fun". He also said, "His ability to concentrate was his greatest asset and his best antidote to anxiety". Just think: he *played* golf; he didn't work at it. Isn't it amazing that many of the highest-paid groups of people on this planet get paid for *playing*! Football and soccer players even play on a *playing* field. In sports, we always ask, "Who is *playing* this weekend?" "Do you know the score of the *game?*" The rest of us go to work to work, not to play. One secret for being successful on a collaborative team is to make what you do a *game* and *play your game*. A common way to describe work is labor, toil, or grind. This way of thinking explains the hell that people have created for themselves by not playing their games. We can maximize play by overcoming obstacles when the outcome of our game is in doubt.

In terms of the game theory, we might say the universe is so constituted to maximize play. The best games are not those in which all goes smoothly and steadily toward a certain conclusion, but those which the outcome is always in doubt.
—George B. Leonard

Overcoming obstacles when your game is not going smoothly gives you the peace of mind, inspiration, and the power to win or reach your goal. Recognizing and overcoming these obstacles gives you a chance to master what some might consider unpleasant circumstances, before they master you. A big win is just a series of small wins that give you a sense of satisfaction and accomplishment to keep going. This gives you a chance to create heaven right here on earth by having fun when you play and enjoy your game.

If our teams, our businesses, our jobs, or our lives are not going smoothly, all we need to do is accept the challenge of taking responsibility to play our game. This will give us new energy and determination to influence the outcome of the game. You can create a fun job right now, even if you don't like the job you have, by changing your attitude from work as toil to finding a way to play your game. Working on a collaborative team that is having fun will automatically lift you into that critical mass that is having fun. When an athlete changes his or her job from play to work, he or she goes downhill fast. Let's find ways to get that 80 percent of the less productive employees to stop working at their jobs and have fun and enjoy their jobs. A collaborative team environment will do that for us.

We need people on our collaborative teams who are willing to look at problems from different perspectives. There is an old Eskimo saying regarding dog sledding that says if you are not lead dog, your view never changes. We need people on our collaborative teams to be able to take the lead dog position when necessary to give the teams new directions.

Another attribute of a good collaborative team member is that of a risk taker. Fear of failure or ruin is what makes most people think that they should avoid risk. Fear is always waiting in the wings to try to derail our creative expressions. We live a life of risks, whether we realize it or not. Nothing worthwhile ever happens without risk to someone. Risk can be looked at as opportunity misspelled, when we apply the right tools to manage that risk. A collaborative team member needs to take the risk of pursuing ideas that others would think impossible. In the judgment phase of a collaborative group process, a team member needs to take the risk of defending and convincing others of his or her minority position when he or she believes the position is right. The biggest risk that anyone can ever take is to never take any risk at all.

Inclusiveness is another important factor in compiling the best collaborative team. Some of the most creative people such as artists, musicians, mathematicians, physicists, engineers, etc., may have had substance abuse, physical or some other problem that would eliminate them from working for most public or private organizations. They may have become stronger through the experiences they have had. These are the experiences that the average good employee may never have had that can bring diversity and invigorating perspective to our blogs. Since blogging can be done off site, there may be a way to include them on a collaborative blogging team. By openly interviewing them and understanding what problems they have had, we may be able to find a way to use their talents and let them know that they could still be part of a collaborative blog team. The more we understand the team members as people, the better we will be able to match the team members who complement each other.

Creative, experienced, and knowledgeable women or men who have left the work force could also be considered for collaborative blog team members since the blogging can be done out of their homes. We don't want to eliminate any possibility of getting the best collaborative team members together. Finding these team members and getting them excited about the blog process and working in a collaborative environment will help us get outstanding results. This will also give the bloggers a chance to grow and have new experiences as they apply their creative talents to management issues.

A collaborative team will come up with more original ideas if it includes people from all walks of life and from all professions and disciplines. People from the same profession or discipline and the same walk of life have had the same experiences. It is difficult for them to come up with original ideas when they are in their own group. However, when they are added to a group that includes diverse backgrounds and experiences, they tend to form a mosaic and stimulate each other to form more original ideas. When the bloggers are anonymous, an idea may be acted on by another blogger who would never have considered it or had given it a second thought if that person knew the social status or the role identity of the original blogger.

Members of a collaborative team need to be able to think for themselves. The ability to think for oneself and develop new ideas is an important attribute of a collaborative team member to have because most of the herd likes to follow.

Have you ever noticed how many people would never start a fight, but the herd instinct makes them willing to jump in as soon as the fight starts? That is why original thinkers are locomotives and the herd is the cars on the journey of life.

The issue of control must be addressed. Functioning on a collaborative team *does not* include control. If you are going to be a good team member, get rid of your need to control and your need to have people behave your way. The first step is to stop dominating and attempting to control, terrorize, and torment those close to you. Then offer to yourself the same escape from the torment and guilt that comes from a control drama. Relax, go with the flow, have some fun and you will be ready for a collaborative team.

Finally, let's look at the attribute of feedback in a collaborative group. My dad built part of the Alcan (Alaska/Canada) highway in 1943 and was away from home for nine months. He and my mother corresponded by letter at least weekly. My mother saved most of his letters and I have read them. In one letter, my mother told my dad that she ran out of gas the other day. He replied in his letter that there was no necessity for him to scold her because experience was a much better teacher than he could ever be. He was just glad that she found a way to get home safely. My dad gave my mother positive feedback. My mother later told me that this feedback changed her emotion from guilt to gratitude for his love and support. Giving positive feedback to those that we work with, including those in our collaborative teams, will lift everyone up, make them more appreciative of each other, and encourage their creativity.

There are never mistakes as long as we look at them as invited lessons. When we recognize a mistake as a learning experience, it provides a momentous new orientation to life. Albert Einstein said, "A person who never made a mistake, never tried anything new". It is the feedback that we get from learning what not to do that teaches us what to do. Feedback makes the learning experience part of our reality. So be gentle with yourself when you have had a learning experience on a collaborative team, have a coffee break, get right back on the team and have some fun!

VI. _Conclusion_

To raise new questions, new possibilities, to regard old questions from a new angle require creative imagination and mark the real advances in science. —Albert Einstein

This book demonstrates that there are new possibilities to look at old questions from a new angle. This new angle requires using a collaborative blog team process, creative imagination, intuition, and problem-solving tools to tap the collective consciousness of organizations. Millions of dollars are spent every year to get outside experts to tell businesses and public agencies what to do and how to think. This outside expert advice is finite and can't compare to the advice of the collective consciousness, which comes from within and is infinite. Creative collective consciousness solutions can come from within by using processes such as a collaborative blog. When we tap the collective consciousness resource of non-productive employees and get them to participate in the process, the process is essentially free. Both the employees' personal lives and contributions they can make to their employers are enhanced.

When the collective consciousness taps the power of the creative imagination of its team members, it becomes possible for anyone to create a vision and communicate and energize that vision with passion to the other team members. The combined energy of imagination and passion in a team will get that vision to take on a life of its own. This is the power that will transform organizations.

Our experiences and thoughts have made us different people than we were last year, ten years ago, or thirty or more years ago. Those people are gone. Experiences and new levels of thought are continually creating a new us with different perspectives, ideas, and belief systems. We need to embrace change, new thoughts, and ideas in order to stimulate growth and expansion in our lives and businesses. Trying to live in the past on old ideas and business principles will only create a slow death. It is change, new experiences, and new thinking that give us new life.

The Roman philosopher Tacitus understood the importance of embracing change and not letting uncertainty and the desire for safety override the need for new experiences and new thinking when he said, "The desire for safety stands against every great and noble enterprise." When we become comfortable with uncertainty and take calculated risks, we will automatically be open to attracting infinite possibilities into our lives and businesses.

Have you ever wondered why some animals don't mate in a zoo? It is because they have no variety and no uncertainty in their lives. They can't embrace life or take risks as they did in the wild. Will Rogers said, "You've got to go out on a limb sometimes because that is where the fruit is". A lack of risk taking and variety when combined with no uncertainty, results in a malaise in most zoo animals. Depression then sets in and that is why they lose interest in mating.

It is amazing to me how many people voluntarily check into the zoo and don't take risks or embrace life and uncertainty. They end up in a trance and wonder why they are so depressed and bored. If they could just get passionate about something or create something or take some risks, they would have a trance-ending experience. It will be the most fun they have experienced since they were kids. Getting people involved in creative collaborative processes will get them out of the zoo and into an arena where they can engage life and have fun on their jobs.

One of the objectives of this book is to show you how to become a deliberate creator of your own experiences in your business or your personal life. We all have extraordinary abilities that can be accessed by the gifts of fantasy such as intuition and imagination. Albert Einstein said, "The gift of fantasy has meant more to me than my talent for absorbing positive knowledge".

Many of us don't realize that some of our thoughts and beliefs are not our own but are put into our heads by others to serve their agendas. We don't have to be walking robots with no idea of what or who is really controlling us in our business or personal lives. We don't have to be slaves to the many stealth mind control groups of the past or present that program our beliefs through fear, repetition of slogans, different forms of hypnosis and autosuggestion. All we have to do is to use the techniques described in this book and we will be free from that kind of slavery and be able to create whatever we want in our lives or businesses. If we want our creations to come more quickly, we can always add more desire, passion and enthusiasm.

I hold the personal belief that we need to share our new ideas with others. This emptying of ourselves by sharing ideas creates a vacuum where newer and better ideas can come in.

Old ideas, like old coffee in a mug, get stale over a period of time. The coffee mug then has no use until it is emptied, cleaned and filled with new coffee. Have you ever considered that no one really drinks coffee? They just borrow it and enjoy the caffeine and the drinking process. Thirty minutes later, they are in the restroom giving the coffee back. Many good things in life, including new ideas from collaborative creative groups, are just like that. We need to have fun and enjoy the process. When something goes well, we can enjoy the moment, give our team members a pat on the back, and then move on and have fun with the process. The nobility of the past enjoyed the foxhunt (process) until the fox got cornered in the tree. Then they moved on because the chase is always more fun than the kill. Once a collaborative team gets involved in a cost reduction or process improvement chase, they will find it more fun and exhilarating than the kill.

These ideas at first may seem strange, but once they are experienced, they can become part of your reality. In the world today, a paradigm shift is just beginning. This shift is a change from depending on experts outside of ourselves to tell us what to think and do, to a new reality of looking within ourselves and our organizations to tell us what to think and do. Jump into this new reality with me and you will not be disappointed. Let's share these ideas with others so that they can experience them. Once we reach a critical mass of people with these ideas, our dreams will be able to be accomplished with minimal physical effort and stress. This will provide the power to lift us all to heights of unimagined satisfaction, in making our businesses and jobs fun and productive, in finding inner peace and joy, and in leading us to experiences that we cannot yet fathom.

Much of the information in this book was obtained by intuition. I focused my thought and demanded to know what

I could say that might be of some benefit to someone even in the smallest way. I let these thoughts go into the universe. This book contains some of the ideas that popped into my mind. I see a vast resource that is waiting to be tapped in the collective consciousness through a collaborative blog process. We are not bound by Pareto's 80/20 law. Let's take his law as a challenge to get the 80 percent of the non-productive people to positively take responsibility to mold their lives and their jobs into something wonderful and exciting. Let's show these people that we can create a positive work environment and put them into a collaborative group where their talents will shine. Let's use the creative blogging process to improve our businesses by engaging people in the creative use of their minds.

The ideas and the techniques in this book will give you wonderful results when a commitment is made to embrace new ideas and change your thinking about your personal life or your business. New ideas and new thoughts bring forth new experiences. These new experiences will create a new reality, which will open you up to a brand new world of possibilities.

Endnotes:

[1] All quotations used in this book are taken from the website "Brainy Quote," which can be located at www.brainyquote.com.

Works Consulted

Haddock, Frank Channing. *Power of Will.* Meridan, CT: The Pelton Publishing Company, 1919.

Mulford, Prentice. *Your Forces, and How to Use Them.* New York: FJ Needham, 1895.

Schwartz, David J. *The Magic of Thinking Big.* New York: Fireside, 1959.

Wattles, Wallace D. *The Science of Getting Rich.* Lakemont, GA: Copple House Books, 1910.

How to use this book

One of the major purposes of this book is for you to have fun reading about how to think and use your creative abilities. This book should be able to be read in a plane, an airport, a home, or any place in a few sittings. I have made it a point to eliminate fluff and to include as many new ideas as possible in a short space so that those of you that are busy interacting with life will have time to read it.

This book can be used as a manual for specific purposes. For example, the introduction and conclusion should be read along with portions of each chapter to meet the following needs:

- How to select and function on a collaborative team: use V, d, and e.

- How to solve business problems: use II, e and III, a, and b.

- How to find the right job: use II, d.

- How to time the stock market: use IV, d and V, c.

- How to improve your personal finances: use II, e, and IV, a, b, c, and e.

- How to be an entrepreneur: entire book.

- How to create what you want in your business or personal life: entire book.

- How to improve your business with creative blogging techniques: entire book

About the Author

Paul William Johnson has spent the last half century as a business executive, an entrepreneur, a stock and commodity trader and an engineer. His main hobbies are music, investing, farming, and crafting and playing reproductions of Renaissance musical instruments. He learned the creative techniques described in this book from his grandmother when he was a teenager. He has successfully used these creative techniques throughout his lifetime in all of his endeavors.

Mr. Johnson has managed cost reduction, process improvement, and value engineering teams for the largest water agency in the world. Mr. Johnson currently provides consulting services to large water agencies, to public agencies and to private businesses. He also participates in value engineering teams. Experiences in all of his endeavors will be shared with you in this book as examples of how you can get your creative intuitive mind to work for you.

Mr. Johnson has been married to his wife, Linda, for forty-five years. They have five children: four are engineers and one is a university professor. They are all directly or indirectly involved in entrepreneurial activities and actively use the creative techniques described in this book. Mr. Johnson wants to share these creative techniques with you so that you can share them with your family, your fellow workers, your employees, and others. There is a great inner peace that comes when you discover that you can create whatever you want in your business or your life.

NOTES

NOTES

NOTES

NOTES

NOTES

NOTES

Printed in the United States
138606LV00002B/84/P